AF228324

COUNTRIES ON THE WORLD STAGE

SPOTLIGHT ON

Germany

Tracy Sue Walker

Lerner Publications ◆ Minneapolis

For Sharon Elaine Walker

Content consultant: Professor Belinda J. Davis, Rutgers University

Lerner Publications Company
An imprint of Lerner Publishing Group, Inc.
241 First Avenue North
Minneapolis, MN 55401 USA

For reading levels and more information, look up this title at www.lernerbooks.com.

Main body text set in Aptifer Sans LT Pro Semibold.
Typeface provided by Linotype AG.

Designer: Athena Currier

Library of Congress Cataloging-in-Publication Data

Names: Walker, Tracy Sue, author.
Title: Spotlight on Germany / Tracy Sue Walker.
Description: Minneapolis : Lerner Publications, [2024] | Series: Countries on the world stage |
    Includes bibliographical references and index. | Audience: Ages 8–12 | Audience: Grades
    4–6 | Summary: "Germany is one of Europe's largest and most powerful nations. Uncover
    Germany's complicated history and look to its future. Then discover the country's key
    leaders, current events, and much more"— Provided by publisher.
Identifiers: LCCN 2022045872 (print) | LCCN 2022045873 (ebook) | ISBN 9781728491981
    (library binding) | ISBN 9798765602546 (paperback) | ISBN 9781728496542 (ebook)
Subjects: LCSH: Germany—Economic conditions—Juvenile literature. | Germany—Politics
    and government—Juvenile literature. | Germany—Population—Juvenile literature. |
    Germany—History—Juvenile literature.
Classification: LCC HC283 .W35 2024 (print) | LCC HC283 (ebook) | DDC 330.943—dc23/
    eng/20230124

LC record available at https://lccn.loc.gov/2022045872
LC ebook record available at https://lccn.loc.gov/2022045873

Manufactured in the United States of America
1-53137-51147-1/19/2023

TABLE OF CONTENTS

Tearing Down the Wall

AFTER NOVEMBER 9, 1989, PEOPLE STARTED CHIPPING PIECES OUT OF THE BERLIN WALL. For the first time in decades, everyone was free to cross the border where the wall once stood. The Berlin Wall had separated Communist East Germany and capitalist West Germany for almost thirty years.

After World War II (1939–1945), Germany was split into different zones. West Germany became the Federal Republic of Germany (FRG). East Germany was the German Democratic Republic (GDR). The city of Berlin was divided between the two and separated by the Berlin Wall. The Berlin Wall's fall started a new era for Germany.

People break off pieces of the Berlin Wall in 1989.

Germany throughout Time

People have lived on the land that is now Germany for thousands of years. Different empires divided and ruled this land for a long time. Several times an empire would try to combine the separate areas only for them to be divided again.

In 1871 Otto von Bismarck unified Germany. He was a conservative politician from Prussia, a German state. Europe was often unstable during this time. Many European countries were at odds with one another because of the power change. World War I (1914–1918) started when

Otto von Bismarck was the first chancellor of the German Empire and served from 1871 to 1890.

Austria-Hungary declared war on Serbia. Germany fought with Austria-Hungary, the Ottoman Empire, and Bulgaria. Germany and its allies fought against France, Britain, Russia, Italy, Japan, and eventually the United States.

About nine million soldiers died during the war. In 1918 Germany lost several battles and its military was weakened. All the other nations fighting in the war had signed an agreement called the Treaty of Versailles to end the war. Germany was the last to sign in 1919.

The agreement said that Germany had to pay the countries it had damaged, give away parts of its territory, and limit its military. Germany had little money after the war. Many Germans were angry that they had to pay other countries. Adolf Hitler and the Nazi Party used people's anger to gain support for their extremist ideas. They hated people who were different from them. They especially targeted Jewish people.

In 1939 Hitler and Germany invaded Poland, which started World War II. Italy and Japan joined Germany in the Axis powers. The Allied powers were led by Britain; the Soviet Union, a former country that included modern-day Russia; and eventually the US.

During World War II, Hitler and the Nazi Party created concentration camps throughout Germany and eastern Europe. Throughout the Holocaust, over six million Jewish people were killed.

REMEMBERING THE HOLOCAUST

Modern Germany honors Holocaust victims. January 27, the day the Auschwitz concentration camp was liberated, is the International Holocaust Remembrance Day. The Memorial to the Murdered Jews of Europe opened in 2005 in Berlin. Additional monuments recognize Jewish victims along with other groups the Nazis targeted, such as Roma and gay people. Many former concentration camps have been turned into museums and memorials as well.

Auschwitz became a museum in 1947 so people could learn about the Holocaust.

Germany finally surrendered in early May 1945. World War II officially ended in the fall of 1945. After World War II, Germany was divided up. In 1949 the two separate states

People gather in West Berlin to support the freeing of East Germany in 1955.

were created. The city of Berlin was also divided. Years later, the Berlin Wall was built to divide east and west.

The United States, Britain, and France controlled capitalist West Germany. The Soviet Union controlled Communist East Germany. Two years after World War II, many countries around the world were fighting again in the Cold War (1947–1991). The Cold War was not a real war. Instead, it was a time of tension between the US and the Soviet Union, but the conflict did lead to smaller wars. The Soviet Union wanted to keep its control of East Germany and prevent Germany from becoming powerful again.

The war was at its peak from 1948 to 1953. During part of this time, the Soviet Union stopped goods from coming into West Berlin. The United States made agreements with other countries to become stronger. In 1955 West Germany joined the agreement with the United States and its allies. By 1961 over two million Germans from East Germany moved to West Germany for more freedom and job opportunities.

In 1955, Chancellor Konrad Adenauer (*center*) supported Germany joining the North Atlantic Trade Organization, an alliance of the US and its allies.

In 1989 and 1990, the Soviet Union began to lose control of Eastern Europe. Soon East Germany became a more democratic country. This led to East and West Germany coming together to create one Germany. Then the Soviet Union broke apart into different countries and the Cold War ended. Over the past thirty years, Germany has come together as one nation.

CHAPTER 2

Exploring Germany

Bordering nine countries, Germany sits in the middle of Europe. More than eighty million people call Germany home. With 134,623 square miles (348,672 sq. km), Germany is one of the most densely populated nations in Europe.

DENMARK
NORTH SEA
BALTIC SEA
NETHERLANDS
Norden
Elbe River
Berlin
POLAND
BELGIUM
Rhine River
GERMANY
CZECH REPUBLIC
LUXEMBOURG
BLACK FOREST REGION
Danube River
FRANCE
Lake Constance
AUSTRIA
SWITZERLAND
Miles
0 25 50 75 100
0 50 100 150
Kilometers
ARCTIC OCEAN
NORTH AMERICA
EUROPE
ASIA
GERMANY
ATLANTIC OCEAN
AFRICA
PACIFIC OCEAN
SOUTH AMERICA
PACIFIC OCEAN
INDIAN OCEAN
AUSTRALIA
SOUTHERN OCEAN
Country capital
International border
Mountains
Norden North (compass)

Heidelberg, Germany, was built
along the Neckar River.

EXPLORE THE RHINE RIVER

The Rhine River flows about 800 miles (1,287 km) past castles and through large cities. It is the most important river in Germany. Goods are shipped up and down its waterways. Small plastic pieces have been found in the river. Low water levels due to climate change also cause harm. Scientists are working on solutions to both problems to improve the health of Germany's most vital river.

Almost 80 percent of people in Germany live in or near cities, with the rest living in rural areas. About one in every ten Germans is an immigrant, helping to make Germany a diverse and culturally vibrant country. Christianity and Islam are major religions in Germany. Other religions practiced in Germany include Judaism, Hinduism, and Buddhism. A majority of people in Germany are ethnically German. People also come from Turkey, Poland, Russia, Romania, and other countries. About eight hundred thousand Germans are Black.

Lakes and mountains blanket the country's south, while low mountains roll into plains in the north. One of Germany's most famous areas, the Black Forest, is in the southwest. Snow-tipped peaks of the Bavarian Alps mountain range rise in the south.

Mighty rivers wind through Germany. The Rhine, the Elbe, and the Weser flow north and empty into the North Sea. Many cities line Germany's rivers, including Heidelberg in the south and Hamburg in the north.

A Powerful Economy

Despite the country's small size, Germany has the world's fourth-largest economy and Europe's largest economy. Its companies lead in many areas, especially in green technologies. This includes products dealing with climate protection and renewable energy.

Machinery and manufacturing make up about a fourth of Germany's economy. This includes the production of chemicals, metals, electrical equipment, automotives, machine tools, textiles, and plastics.

Twenty-two percent more solar panels were installed in Germany in the first six months of 2022 than in the first six months of 2021.

EXPLORE GERMAN ENGINEERING

Engineers use math and science to create and build structures. Germany is famous for its engineering. Many carmakers are German companies such as Porsche and Mercedes-Benz. They build some of their cars in Germany.

A German engineer builds a car engine in 2022.

Farming is an important part of the German economy. Germany is also the largest milk producer in the European Union (EU). The EU is an alliance between many European countries.

In addition, German agriculture includes the production of potatoes, sugar beets, oilseeds, fruits, and vegetables.

While there are large corporations and businesses in Germany, smaller businesses are plentiful too. These small and medium-sized companies are often owned and operated by families over many generations. These companies employ 80 percent of the nation's workforce.

CHAPTER 4

One United Government

Germany has a written constitution known as the Basic Law. The Basic Law was already in effect in West Germany when unification took place in 1990. On October 3, 1990, the Basic Law was adopted by a united Germany.

German citizens vote for some of their leaders. Every citizen who participates in elections gets to cast two votes. The first vote is for local representation. The second is for

A voter submits their ballot in Berlin, Germany.

parliamentary representation. Only German citizens who are at least eighteen years old can vote in these elections. Some citizens with a criminal record may not be permitted to vote.

Germany has two houses of parliament: the Bundestag and the Bundesrat. The Bundestag represents all of Germany. Members pass laws. The Bundesrat represents the country's sixteen states. Bundesrat's representatives are not elected. They represent the ruling political majority of each state. The chancellor leads the executive branch.

Germany's judiciary enforces laws. The Federal Constitutional Court is the only court that can declare legislation unconstitutional. Judges in this court serve a single, nonrenewable, twelve-year term. Half the members are elected by the Bundesrat, and half are elected by a special committee of the Bundestag.

The Bundestag meets in 2022.

DISCOVER THE CHANCELLOR OF GERMANY

The chancellor heads Germany's executive branch. They are elected by the Bundestag and then form their cabinet. The cabinet's ministers help the chancellor govern Germany. The chancellor decides on policies for the government.

Chancellor Olaf Scholz attends a conference in 2022.

There are many political parties in Germany. Parties often do not have a majority in the legislature, so they form coalitions with other parties. These coalitions work together to achieve common goals.

Modern Germany

REMNANTS OF THE WALL THAT DIVIDED EAST AND WEST BERLIN ARE STILL VISIBLE IN PARTS OF THE CITY. They are a constant reminder to the German people of the turmoil and struggles of the past. But they are also a reminder of how much the country has evolved.

Angela Merkel served as chancellor from 2005 to 2021. Olaf Scholz became Germany's new chancellor in 2021.

A year later, Russia invaded its neighboring country, Ukraine. Germany uses Russian gas for its energy. Germany began to get more of its gas from other countries, but it still buys some gas from Russia. Some of Germany's allies don't want it to buy gas from Russia because they worry Russia will use the money to attack Ukraine.

Germany has faced many challenges over the years. It will continue to face them, and how it responds will shape the country and the world.

Germans look forward to the future of their country.

TIMELINE

500 BCE–100 CE People settle in the area now known as Germany.

800 Charlemagne becomes emperor of Germany.

1024–1125 German princes rise to power.

1871 Germany unites as the German Empire.

1914–1918 Germany fights in World War I until its defeat.

1933 Adolf Hitler rises to power.

1939–1945 Germany fights in World War II until its defeat.

1945 The Yalta Conference decides to divide Germany into different zones.

1990 West and East Germany unite to become the Federal Republic of Germany.

2021 Olaf Scholz becomes chancellor of Germany after Angela Merkel steps down.

2022 A pipeline that sends gas from Russia to Germany is attacked.

FAST FACTS

Official name: Federal Republic of Germany

Population: 80,457,737

Land area: 134,623 square miles (348,672 sq. km)

Largest city: Berlin

Capital city: Berlin

Form of government: federal republic

Official language: German

Flag:

GLOSSARY

cabinet: a group of people who act as advisers

capitalist: an advocate of capitalism, an economic system where citizens own and run companies to make money

coalition: people or groups with different goals or ideas working together for a shared goal

Communist: an advocate of communism, an economic system where the government owns the means of production

concentration camp: a type of prison where large numbers of people are held against their will

constitution: a set of rules that guides how a country works

economy: the process or systems in which goods and services are produced, sold, and bought in a country

empire: a group of countries or regions controlled by one ruler or one government

federal republic: a state or a union of states that does not have a monarch

Holocaust: the killing of millions of Jews and other people by the Nazis during World War II

policy: a set of rules or a plan used to guide action

LEARN MORE

Britannica Kids: Germany
https://kids.britannica.com/kids/article/Germany/345694

Coddington, Andrew, and Sloane Gould. *Germany*. New York: Cavendish Square, 2023.

Cool Kid Facts: Germany
https://www.coolkidfacts.com/germany-facts-for-kids/

Foran, Racquel. *Germany*. Minneapolis: Abdo, 2023.

Kids World Travel Guide: Germany Facts
https://www.kids-world-travel-guide.com/germany-facts.html

Layton, Christine. *Travel to Germany*. Minneapolis: Lerner Publications, 2023.

National Geographic Kids: Germany
https://kids.nationalgeographic.com/geography/countries/article/germany

Walker, Tracy Sue. *Spotlight on Russia*. Minneapolis: Lerner Publications, 2024.

INDEX

PHOTO ACKNOWLEDGMENTS

Image credits: Sueddeutsche Zeitung Photo/Alamy Stock Photo, p. 5; Photo by London Stereoscopic Company/Hulton Archive/Getty Images, p. 7; Photo by © Hulton-Deutsch Collection/CORBIS/Getty Images, p. 8; Culture Club/Getty Images, p. 9; Artur Widak/NurPhoto/Getty Images, p. 10; SuperStock/Alamy Stock Photo, p. 11; World History Archive/Alamy Stock Photo, p. 12; dpa/picture alliance/Getty Images, p. 13; Laura Westlund/Independent Picture Service, p. 15; Kanuman/Shutterstock, p. 16; Marina Lohrbach/iStock/Getty Images, p. 19; Tim Graham/Alamy Stock Photo, p. 20; Thorsten Schier/Shutterstock, p. 21; Sean Gallup/Getty Images, p. 23; Michael Kappeler/picture alliance/Getty Images, p. 24; Islam Safwat/Bloomberg/Getty Images, p. 25; Aliaksandr Antanovich/Shutterstock, p. 27.

Cover: canadastock/Shutterstock.